DEVILISH DETAILS

Developing the new Framework for Achievement

Peter Wilson

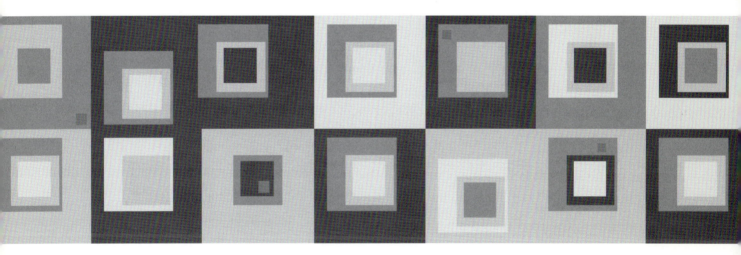

A Policy Discussion Paper

niace
promoting adult learning

DEVILISH DETAILS

Developing the new
Framework for Achievement

A Policy Discussion Paper

Peter Wilson

niace
promoting adult learning

Published by the National Institute of
Adult Continuing Education (England and Wales)

21 De Montfort Street
Leicester LE1 7GE
Company registration no. 2603322
Charity registration no. 1002775

First published 2004

niace
promoting adult learning

NIACE has a broad remit to promote lifelong learning
opportunities for adults. NIACE works to develop
increased participation in education and training,
particularly for those who do not have easy access
because of barriers of class, gender, age, race,
language and culture, learning difficulties and
disabilities, or insufficient financial resources.

www.niace.org.uk

Cataloguing in Publication Data
A CIP record of this title is available from the British Library

Designed and typeset by Boldface, London
Printed in Great Britain by Newnorth, Bedford

ISBN 1 86201 221 0

Foreword

A NIACE policy discussion paper aims to create a debate about a matter of national importance. This paper comes at a crucial time. The Government's commitment to a credit framework for adults was signalled in the Skills Strategy White Paper in July 2003. The Qualifications and Curriculum Authority together with the Learning and Skills Council have moved on this at a good pace. It is appropriate that a key adviser in this process is the author of this paper.

Peter Wilson identifies key technical issues involved in a credit framework for adults such as unit recognition, the relationship between and units and credit value and rules of combination for achievement of qualifications. He argues that an inclusive national qualifications framework is a 'very practical proposition' and not just a theoretical dream. Peter concludes that there are many variables to be drawn together. Creating an inclusive Framework for Achievement while at the same time maintaining the stability of credits as 'a currency of achievement' is hard enough. To do so and to make a framework that is intelligible to all users and potential users seems very hard indeed.

This paper shows some ways in which an inclusive Framework for Achievement can be realised. If all those who work in this area were half as clear in their explanation of how it could work as this author, some policy makers would feel a lot less anxious about a new framework, let alone qualifications and what they stand for.

Peter Lavender
Director (Research)
NIACE

A new beginning...

One year on from the publication of the July 2003 White Paper *21st Century Skills: Realising our potential* our initial surprise at the contents of Chapter 5 has subsided.[1] The paper included commitments previously signalled in other documents, together with a number of 'tidying up' proposals designed to sweep several areas of reform into a single strategic overview – the Skills Strategy. Among this raft of measures was a simple and clear commitment to develop 'a credit framework for adults' as a central plank for reform of the qualifications system in England.

Following publication of the White Paper the Department for Education and Skills (DfES) moved quickly to commission both the Qualifications and Curriculum Authority (QCA) and the Learning and Skills Council (LSC) to take forward this commitment. Although QCA and LSC are now working to a single joint remit, QCA is leading work on the technical development of a reformed National Qualifications Framework (NQF) based on a credit system, while LSC is working to ensure that this system encompasses achievements that currently sit outside the NQF.

Some months after the acceptance of their joint remit from the DfES, it is clear that QCA and LSC are working closely together[2] on this key development and a mood of optimism prevails. Nevertheless the question of the relationship between 'credit inside' and 'credit outside' the NQF remains as an issue to be resolved through the next phase of development. This paper will suggest that confronting these perceptions of 'inside' and 'outside' in relation to credit is the key to understanding how the practical process of implementing the Skills Strategy commitment to qualifications reform should now proceed.

...or another false dawn?

Although the commitment to an adult credit framework in *21st Century Skills* came as a surprise, the arguments for such a development have been around for some time. It is worth a few moments to dip in to this 'brief history of credit' in order to understand how the past might help us to make sense of the future. In so doing we also need to confront the possibility that some elements of this past may be a hindrance to us in taking forward the development of credit in this new context.

We may trace the origins of the idea of a national credit framework back to initial discussion papers developed through the South Yorkshire Open College Federation in the late 1980s, through a Further Education Staff College Paper workshop on 'Modularisation and Credit' in 1990,[3] and then to a conference in November 1991 entitled 'Towards a National Credit Framework'.[4] In February 1992 the Further Education Unit (FEU) released 'A Basis for Credit?'[5] and the early 1990s saw the rapid adoption of the call for a national credit framework across the post-school sector. A decade before the publication of *21st Century Skills* the call for a national credit framework was supported by a wide range of representative bodies, from the Association for Colleges to the Headmasters Conference.[6] Local and regional credit frameworks sprang up in many areas, and the array of local Open College Networks (OCNs) grew rapidly into a national presence.

At the same time central Government remained distinctly unresponsive to these demands. The National Council for Vocational Qualifications (NCVQ) pronounced itself not in favour of a credit framework. Its submission to a parliamentary committee on the subject was unequivocal in its view that 'credit' was a potential threat to 'standards'.[7] It should also be recalled that, even a decade ago, qualifications were primarily things for young people. The idea that adults might also seek recognition for their achievements was only beginning to creep into mainstream policy for the post-school sector. The call for a national credit framework remained a grass-roots idea, ignored by policy makers.

But it was an idea that would not go away. FEU and then its successor, the Further Education Development Agency (FEDA), continued to advocate the idea of a credit framework.[8] The National Open College Network (NOCN) continued to expand rapidly throughout the 1990s.[9] Both the Kennedy[10] and Fryer[11] reports of the mid-1990s contained explicit recommendations for a national credit framework as a vehicle for widening participation and creating a more inclusive FE sector. Amidst these continuing calls for development of a national credit framework however, an alternative path of reform was unfolding, and it is this separate strand that now needs to be considered.

The development of a National Qualifications Framework

The establishing of a National Qualifications Framework (NQF) was a recommendation of the Dearing report on qualifications for 16-19 year-olds in 1996.[12] The Education Act of the following year created the NQF and the regulatory authorities that were charged with responsibility to bring it into being.[13] The concept of a national framework within which all qualifications would be located is therefore a much newer and less well-established idea than that of a national credit framework, within which all achievements of learners could be represented.

The expressed intention of the initial NQF was that it would be 'inclusive' in character. In other words when the NQF was fully established it would include all qualifications and these qualifications would be the sole structures within which learner achievements (outside Higher Education) would be recognised. When the structure of the NQF was established in 1998 it was envisaged that this period of development would take up to five years. In other words by 2003 the NQF would encompass all recognised achievements within formally-approved qualifications.

The reality, of course, is spectacularly different. The NQF encompasses most qualifications offered to 16-19 year-olds in full-time education, but these learners make up a little over 15% of the total number of learners now supported in their learning activities by the Learning and Skills Council (LSC). When LSC-supported learners over the age of 19 are considered, a small minority of these are studying towards a qualification within the NQF. Indeed, even when those who are not registered for any form of certification are excluded, some 75% of adult learners are enrolled on programmes leading to an award outside the NQF.[14] Whatever its intentions, the structures of the NQF and the procedures for approval of qualifications within it have created major barriers to the development of an inclusive framework.

We should not be so surprised by this failure of the NQF to achieve its intention to become 'inclusive' of all learning achievements. Its structural origins lay in the recommendations of a report focused explicitly on the needs of 16-19 year olds. Institutionally, the regulatory authorities were formed through the fusing of two organisations (NCVQ and SCAA – the Schools Curriculum and Assessment Authority) that between them had responsibility for approval of qualifications offered to less than 20% of learners in the then Further Education sector. The ability of QCA and its partner authorities in Wales and Northern Ireland to encompass the range of recognised achievements offered to learners across the whole post-school sector was always a challenge to their structures and to their particular history. The quinquennial review of QCA in 2002 confirmed these shortcomings.[15]

The changed context of the 21st century

At around the same time that the NQF was being established, the (still relatively new) Labour Government issued a further pronouncement on a national credit framework. The then minister for Lifelong Learning, Baroness Blackstone, wrote to the new Chair of the QCA, declaring the Government 'interested' in the possible benefits of a credit framework for adult learners, and invited the Authority to undertake further work to establish what these benefits might be and how they might be implemented within the remit of QCA.[16]

The 'Blackstone letter' was interesting in that, for the first time, it located future responsibility for the development of a credit framework in the hands of an organisation with responsibility for regulating qualifications (rather than a development agency). It also made it clear that the Government remained to be convinced about the benefits of a credit framework, and that much further work needed to be done by QCA before any formal blessing for such a development might emanate from Whitehall.

Then began a period of 'further work' by QCA, which proceeded slowly and modestly over several years without ever arriving at a positive (or negative) recommendation to Government about the efficacy of establishing a credit framework for adults. This period, from 1998 to 2003, also saw the gradual scaling down or winding up of many of the local and regional initiatives that had sprung up in the early 1990s in response to the initial calls to establish a national credit framework.[17] The dramatic increase in the growth of OCNs and NOCN began to slow down.[18] and the previously active role of bodies like LSDA and NIACE in supporting credit-based developments became a passive and more marginal activity.[19] By 2002, ten years on from the publication of *A Basis for Credit?* it was clear that the grass-roots movement that had grown up behind the call for establishing of a national credit framework was in decline.

It was this same year (2002) when the A/AS level debacle of that summer led to the crisis in the QCA and the resignation of both its Chief Executive and later the Secretary of State for Education.[20] Following on the criticisms of the quinquennial review and the DfES's review of QCA's remit, it became clear that significant reform of the NQF was now to be expected. A new Chief Executive was appointed to QCA with a clear brief to undertake radical reform of the NQF.[21] The establishing of the Tomlinson Committee[22] and the publication of the Skills Strategy White Paper in July 2003 set the context of government support for these reforms, with the commitment to a credit framework for adults an explicit part of this context.

We may therefore postulate that it has been the manifest failings of the NQF, rather than the inexorable growth of credit systems outside the NQF, that has persuaded the Government to commit itself to the development of a credit framework for adults. In fact it is probably not too exaggerated to imagine that 'credit' may well have disappeared from view in the coming years as a 'big idea' in the post-school sector that had never quite made it into official policy. It remains to be seen how the next period of development will unfold, but it seems as though the idea of a credit framework has been rehabilitated just in time to ensure that its implementation can be based on existing practice and experience rather than distant memories.

A national credit framework?

As we note above, the key features of a national credit framework were developed many years before the establishing of the NQF. Most of these features were based on the framework developed by OCNs and formalised within NOCN in the early 1990s.[23] As such they were developed without reference to existing qualifications, and indeed much work on credit was developed as an explicit adult-focused alternative to the more traditional and less flexible qualifications designed for 16-19 year-olds in full-time education.

The concept of credit developed in the post-school sector over the last twenty years has never consciously attempted to present itself as a type of qualification. The model for credit is derived as much from traditions of course accreditation in Higher Education as it is from the development of either academic or vocational qualifications for 16-19 year-olds. Thus providers developed programmes of learning, often specific to a single institution, and these programmes offered assessment leading to the award of credit.[24] Credit-based provision has always been responsive to particular needs and is capable of great flexibility in recognising many different kinds of achievement.

Conversely, the specifications of the credit framework developed during the 1990s created structures which did not lend themselves easily to national measures of comparability, to centrally-developed approaches to assessment, or to the creation of nationally-recognised 'exchange values' for credits as the representation of achievements that would trigger progression opportunities. The practical development of credit-bearing programmes also led to accusations of inefficiency and unnecessary duplication that were in part justified.

By 1997 and the creation of the NQF, the limitations of the concept of 'a national credit framework' were beginning to become clear. If there was to be such a thing as an NQF then all achievements that were recognised outside this framework would be seen as in some way diminished by exclusion. From this point in time the idea that a national credit framework might be sanctioned by central government and developed as an alternative framework for recognising achievement became an untenable proposition. If the concept of a national credit framework was going to survive into the 21st century, it had to find an accommodation with the concept of an NQF.

The location of the commitment to develop a credit framework for adults within the wider context of reform of qualifications therefore presents an opportunity to take forward the development of credit within an overall review of recognising learner achievement in the post-school sector. It is suggested that this is an opportunity not to be missed, but it requires some creative forgetting, as well as remembering, among those previously involved in calls for the development of a national credit framework.

Two ideas in search of each other

Despite the explicit reference to a credit framework in *21st Century Skills* it is suggested that the bringing together of the concepts of 'credit framework' and 'qualifications framework' will prove unnecessarily problematic. What is needed instead is the conscious development of a different type of qualification within a reformed NQF that is based on the key specifications of credit. Now that the further development of a credit framework is linked explicitly to the wider context of qualifications reform, we should be prepared to abandon the concept of 'a national credit framework' within a renewed commitment to credit-based qualifications within a new national framework for recognising achievement.

This reform of the NQF is already under way within an overall commitment to the recognition of learner achievement within a new framework. Indeed the formalisation of this reform under the heading of the Framework for Achievement (FfA) is itself a major step forward.[25] It is suggested here that the incorporation of the specifications of credit into this new Framework will provide the key to reform of qualifications that can deliver on the renewed intention of QCA that the framework should be 'inclusive' in respect of learner achievements. It may also enable us, in time, to dissolve the ideas of 'credit inside' and 'credit outside' the NQF into a single, inclusive framework of credit-based qualifications.

In summary then, both the credit framework and the NQF need each other. Without the transition from 'credit framework' to 'credit-based qualifications' the further development of credit cannot proceed as a genuinely national system. Similarly, without the insertion of credit into the architecture of the NQF, our qualifications system cannot transform itself into an inclusive Framework for Achievement.

This paper suggests that the bringing together of these two different traditions of credit and the NQF can create the technical architecture necessary to transform our qualifications system into a genuinely inclusive structure for recognising achievement. This is a challenging agenda but a realisable goal. In order to make progress towards this goal some key issues need to be resolved. This paper goes on to identify some of these key issues and to propose ways in which this architecture of credit-based qualifications within a reformed NQF can now be developed.

An architecture for a credit system

Once the different concepts of 'credit framework' and 'qualifications framework' are no longer competing for the same ideological or technical space, it becomes possible to develop a concept of 'systems architecture' for credit-based qualifications. This architecture may be described as an interconnected set of technical specifications that will permit the effective operation of a system of credit accumulation and transfer to underpin qualifications within a national framework.

This paper suggests that it is now necessary to reach agreement on some of the key features of this architecture in order to guarantee the smooth and effective operation of a credit system leading to qualifications. Some of these key architectural features are described below, while the later sections of this paper try to illustrate how a credit system might function within these features.

Very little of this architecture is 'new'. The features described below have been developed over a number of years within existing credit systems in both HE and the Learning and Skills sector. Nor does this paper attempt to describe a comprehensive set of technical features for credit-based qualifications. Some key features are identified which, it is suggested, will be an essential underpinning for an effectively functioning credit system leading to qualifications.

Some operational principles

Before describing these key specifications it is necessary to identify some of the desired features of an operational system of credit-based qualifications. Thus the systems architecture needs to be designed in such a way as to enable these operational principles to function smoothly and efficiently. Some of these operational principles are clearly signalled in *21st Century Skills*. Others reflect the remits for development of a credit framework given to QCA and LSC. Some are also derived from existing practice within credit systems.

The following four principles are suggested as the basis for system design:

- all credits awarded to learners should be able to count towards at least one qualification within the FfA;
- there should be no distinction between different types of credit (eg 'adult credits', '14-19 credits', 'vocational credits' etc.). All credits awarded should be capable of inclusion within the achievement requirements of all qualifications;
- all credits should be transferable in principle between all qualifications offered by any awarding body;
- all qualifications should be based on an explicit set of rules that set out the opportunities for and limitations on credit accumulation and transfer.

The application of these principles to a system of credit-based qualifications will, it is suggested, lead to the maximum level of inclusion, flexibility and responsiveness in recognising learner achievement. In order for this system to operate effectively it will be necessary to establish a stable and robust set of technical specifications to support it. These specifications will collectively become the architecture of the qualifications framework.

The key features of the architecture and system for recognising achievement

In developing these features it will be necessary to draw on the experiences of both practice in existing credit systems and on the existing features of the NQF. Thus although the combination of specifications will be particular to the purposes of supporting an inclusive system of credit-based qualifications, each individual specification will be known to practitioners in the learning and skills sector.

It is suggested that the following will be critical 'pressure points' in a future system of credit-based qualifications, and that therefore it will be important to establish a particular architectural feature to ensure that the principles outlined above continue to inform the development of the FfA. These are:

- the specification of the unit;
- the relationship between units and credit value;
- the rules of combination for qualifications.

The following paragraphs deal with each of these features in turn. A subsequent set of paragraphs will then address three key operational processes that are derived from these specifications. These processes are:

- admitting units to a national databank;
- establishing and approving rules of combination;
- accumulating and transferring credits towards a qualification.

Although there are many other points of technical detail to be resolved in developing this framework of credit-based qualifications, it is suggested that if each of the above features can be established to support the principles previously outlined, then other details can follow consistently.

The unit specification

Although there are examples of credit systems that operate without a relationship to units, over the past two decades in the UK all operational credit systems in both HE and the Learning and Skills sector have based themselves explicitly on a common unit specification. The *Credit Principles for England* document produced by QCA[26] to support its work on credit adopts the accepted specifications of a unit in use across credit systems throughout the UK. We may therefore state with confidence that a unit has the following specification:

- a title;
- a set of learning outcomes;
- a related set of assessment criteria;
- a level;
- a credit value.

It is also suggested that a unit will also need to have a unique code, but we may treat this as a secondary feature.

Having established that this is the agreed unit specification that will underpin a system of credit-based qualifications, it is necessary to assert some of the features of the architecture for this credit system that follow from this specification. The following statements flow logically from this assertion:

- only units with this specification may lead to the award of credit;
- no additional specifications may be added to the standard unit format;
- only credits awarded in relation to units conforming to this specification may count towards a qualification.

We therefore need to recognise that previous developments taking place under the banner of 'unitisation' may not conform to these particular specifications. As the particular format of the unit is critical to the stability of credit values in the architecture of the framework, any attempt to ascribe credit values to units that do not conform to these specifications would be a potential threat to the credit as a consistent representation of the currency of learner achievement.

In order to protect the consistency of the credit it is therefore necessary for a single unit specification to be established by the body or bodies responsible for regulating the credit system. This will also be a necessary part of the arrangements for setting up a national unit databank. As an early step towards developing an operational credit system the regulatory authorities therefore need to establish a standard electronic format for the unit, based on the specifications above, and make this freely available to all who wish to use it.

The relationship between units and credit value

It now seems clear that the basis for determining credit values in the new framework for recognising achievement will be 10 learning hours. It is not the purpose of this paper to debate the merits of this particular figure. However it should be noted that a 10-hour basis for determining credit values is a largely untested figure. Over the past two decades credit systems have developed in the Learning and Skills sector on the basis of credit values based on 30 learning hours. Although the 10-hour basis for credit value is used by many universities there are no examples of HE institutions committing themselves to the award of credit (rather than the ascribing of a numerical value to part of a programme) based on this definition of credit value.

The argument for a 10-hour basis for calculating credit values has usually been based on the not unreasonable assumption that, in certain instances, learners may seek recognition of their achievements after 10 hours of learning. Although this may be true, it is also the case that the lower the figure used as the basis for calculating credit values of units, the higher the risk of instability in the currency of credit and the greater the risk of a high-cost assessment regime. How then might we balance the need to offer learners a sensitive measure of their achievements with the demands for stability in the overall system of calculating credit values, accepting the 10-hour basis for this calculation?

Two simple devices are proposed. These devices reflect established practice in all HE credit systems and in the Scottish Credit and Qualifications Framework (SCQF):[27]

- to limit the permitted credit values of units;
- to develop rules of combination for qualifications based on these limited credit values.

In order to underwrite the consistency of credit values necessary to support a stable architecture for the new Framework, and to facilitate the smoothest possible transition from existing credit systems, the following permitted credit values of units within credit-based qualifications are proposed:

One   Two   Three   Six   Nine   Twelve

These limitations may be further refined by developing slightly different limits for units at different levels. So, for example, the permitted range of credit values for units at Entry Level might be one, two, three and six. At Level Four these values might be three, six, nine and 12. (Again this relationship between level and credit values is part of the SCQF). These are the kind of details that can be established through consultation in the future.

One reason for proposing these limitations on credit values is that we need to anticipate the process through which credit values will be ascribed to units within the proposed framework. There is a consensus among those organisations involved in developing credit-based qualifications that this must be a responsibility of the bodies that award credit to learners. This seems an entirely practical proposition. In these circumstances it would be very difficult to ascribe credit values accurately to larger units if any multiple of such values was permitted. Could we really guarantee that the process of ascribing a credit value of, for example, 10 to one unit could establish that figure clearly in relation to a credit value of 11 ascribed to another unit? Such claims for accuracy in the ascribing of credit values would surely be spurious.

These limitations on permitted credit values could be changed over time in response to identified demand and the growing maturity of the credit system. However it is suggested that in the first instance the limitations proposed above would be an important part of guaranteeing the stability of the credit as the basis for recognising learner achievements.

A related technical feature of this architecture is proposed:

- All qualifications should be based on rules of combination of credit values that are divisible by three.

This would mean that the smallest qualification would have a credit value of three, though this could be made up of one, two or three units, with credit available to learners for the achievement of any of these units. It is suggested that this limitation at one end of the spectrum of achievement would produce benefits throughout the overall framework as the rules of accumulation and transfer of credit would be based on a less complex and more accessible relationship between units and qualifications than one in which any multiple of credit value was permitted.

The rules of combination for qualifications

In order that the details of individual qualifications can be communicated easily to users, it is suggested that a standardised structure for presenting rules of combination for achievement of qualifications is developed. These rules would be based on explicit limitations and opportunities for the accumulation and transfer of credit. (The term 'based on' is used here as it would be possible to set additional requirements for the achievement of a qualification that fell outside these rules for credit accumulation and transfer, for example in relation to grading).

This structure could be developed straightforwardly through consultation based on existing examples of such rules of combination. Through these rules of combination a spectrum of different types of limitations and opportunities for credit accumulation and transfer could be described that were appropriate to the particular purpose of the qualification. Thus, although credit-based qualifications offer the basis for very open and flexible rules of combination to be developed, in certain instances a highly restricted set of rules might be appropriate.

The following statements illustrate the range of different types of statement that would make up a set of rules of combination for any individual qualification. Some variation on these statements could be developed in a logical sequence for every qualification within the framework:

Requirement	Comments
The qualification will be awarded for the achievement of z credits	Sets out the overall credit value of the qualification
Of these, a minimum of y credits must be achieved at Level x	Sets out the requirement for credit achievement at the level of the qualification
All other credits must be achieved at Level w	Sets out subsidiary rules for credit achievement
Of the y credits at Level x, v must be achieved from the core units	Sets out the requirements for achievement in the core units and includes reference to a list of core units
Outside the core, a minimum of u credits must be achieved at Levels x or w from the optional units	Sets limitations on the accumulation of credits from optional units and includes a reference to a list of these units
All remaining credits must be drawn from units in classes t, s, r or q of the unit classification system	Refers to limitations on credits from outside those listed in the qualification and refers to the QCA subject classification system
A maximum of n credits at Level x may be transferred from another qualification or qualifications	Limits opportunities for credit transfer at the level of the qualification
There are no limitations on the transfer of credit from other qualifications at Level w	Sets an open rule for credit transfer at the lower level of credit achievement
A maximum of m credits at Level x may be exempted from credit achievement on the basis of other qualifications	Sets limits on exemption from credit achievement on the basis of non-credit-based qualifications and refers to a list of credit equivalences for such qualifications.

Of course some rules of combination might be very simple, especially where options and opportunities for credit transfer are limited. However, as the range of credit-based qualifications in any one subject or occupational area grows, the opportunities for developing creative opportunities for utilising the potential of a credit system will also begin to grow, and we may anticipate that awarding bodies will create more open and flexible rules of combination for newer qualifications.

Operational procedures

Having suggested how three key technical specifications might be established, we now turn to suggest how three operational features of a credit system might be developed. In putting forward these suggestions, we seek to maximise the responsiveness and flexibility of credit-based qualifications within an overall set of procedures that are manageable for awarding bodies and comprehensible to users.

A national unit databank

One of the key phrases in the references to a credit framework in *21st Century Skills* is that there should be 'mutual recognition of units' within such a framework. This will play an important role in the development of both efficiency and flexibility in credit-based qualifications, and it is suggested that the establishing of a national unit databank will be a critical basis for this mutual recognition. The following features of such a databank, and the admission of units to it, are suggested.

The databank is conceived as an electronic store of key information about credit-based qualifications. The technology for establishing a web-based databank and creating easy access to it is now widely available. Indeed there are existing models of such databanks that could be drawn on in such a development, including QCA's own OpenQuals database.[28]

One of the key technical requirements for such a databank is referred to above: the establishing of a standard technical format for all units admitted to the databank. It should be emphasised again here that the primary rationale for establishing a standard unit format is to support the consistent ascribing of credit values to units. Nevertheless, there will be a number of benefits to users of credit-based qualifications in the establishing of this shared electronic format for units.

One of the features of the NQF that has been most criticised is the time taken by the regulatory authorities to approve individual qualifications. Indeed QCA has already made significant changes in its processes of approval to address this problem.[29] It is suggested that the process of admission of units to this national databank needs to be as open as possible in order to avoid 'approval bottlenecks'. It will certainly not be appropriate for each individual unit to be subject to individual scrutiny and approval by the regulator(s) of the FfA.

As part of the development of revised accreditation criteria for approval of qualifications in the FfA, it is therefore suggested that responsibility for placing units in a national databank should be a responsibility that rests primarily with awarding bodies. Although there may be circumstances (eg. units developed in response to a central Government strategy like *Skills for Life*) where units may be placed on the database through an alternative route, it is suggested that only awarding bodies or the regulator itself may place units within the databank. This will not, of course, prevent awarding bodies commissioning unit development from other agencies, or for reaching agreements with employers or other third parties on the development of units to be placed in the databank. But, in order to guarantee the integrity of the systems architecture, the regulator(s) of the Framework must be able to monitor and assure themselves of the quality of the process through which units are placed in the databank.

Devolving this responsibility to awarding bodies will require the regulator to ensure that there are effective procedures in place to ensure the quality of units placed in the databank, and the consistency with which the technical features of these units (particularly in relation to the ascribing of level and credit value) are established. It is suggested that such responsibilities are entirely consistent with the revisions of accreditation criteria for admission of qualifications to the NQF that the regulatory authorities are now piloting.

In order to function effectively, a unit databank would be made freely and openly accessible to all users. The logical consequence of this is that, in submitting units to the databank, awarding bodies would cede ownership of these units to the regulating authority. The regulators would effectively hold the copyright of units 'in stewardship' on behalf of all users of the databank.

This conception of units as 'public goods' will also be necessary to protect the interests of Sector Skills Councils. Many of the units admitted to the databank will be based on occupational standards developed by an SSC and these standards are required to be treated as 'public goods'. It would therefore be both illogical and impractical for awarding bodies (or any other organisation) to claim 'ownership' of a unit based on standards that themselves were not susceptible to such a claim.

In relation to SSCs, it is assumed that one of the criteria for admission of units to the databank in particular occupational areas would be a requirement that the SSC supported their admission. Awarding bodies would need to secure such support as part of the process of placing relevant units in the databank, and these processes would be subject to scrutiny by the regulator. Thus support from an SSC (or other designated standards-setting body) would be an important part of the process of rationalising the development of the unit databank. Such requirements would, it is assumed, form a natural part of an overall Sector Qualifications Strategy.[30]

This would not be the only mechanism for rationalisation however. A more powerful control in the longer term would be the free and open access to all units within the databank for all awarding bodies. Thus in the development and updating of any qualification, the starting point for development would be a search of the unit databank for appropriate units that the awarding body could use. Where no appropriate units were available, new units would be developed. Thus the databank functions both to support an efficient process of qualifications development, and as a motor for continuous improvement and updating of units in response to demand.

An openly accessible unit databank will also serve as a guarantor of the stability of credit values over time. There will be no advantages to be gained by any one awarding body in placing units on the databank with a perceived 'high' or 'low' credit value in relation to similar units, as these units would be available to all other awarding bodies. We may assume that, as new units are developed over time and older units cease to be used, credit values will become gradually more stable and the credit itself more secure as a currency of achievement.

In order to establish effective processes for the admission of units to the databank, the process of qualification approval needs to be separated from the admission of units to the databank. Although the regulator will have a role as a 'moderator' of the databank and will be responsible for the development of continuous guidance on unit development to support the process of quality improvement of units, it is suggested that there should be no formal 'approval gateway' to the databank (eg. a central 'Approvals Committee' or similar body) that is controlled by the regulator, other than the technical specifications of the above unit format.

Thus approval of qualifications can be focused more efficiently on the rules of combination for qualifications, linked to the use of particular qualification titles, rather than on approval of individual units. It will be sufficient to require any unit referred to in any rule of combination to be placed in the databank in order to secure an active and continuing process of admission and replacement of units in the databank.

Approving rules of combination

As the above sections of this paper imply, there will be three key procedures through which the regulator(s) of the Framework for Achievement can exercise the controls over the approval of credit-based qualifications that will be necessary to support the stability of the credit as a currency of achievement within a system that is both efficient and responsive to changing needs.

The most important of these will be the process for approving the processes of individual awarding bodies as providing sufficient guarantees of quality in the conduct of assessment leading to the award of credit. The second will be the process of admitting units to a national databank. The third will be the approval of the 'rules of combination' for individual qualifications.

It is suggested that the format for presenting rules of combination outlined above will provide a straightforward and effective structure within which a regulator can quickly approve a named qualification. One of the primary benefits of a system of credit-based qualifications would be that the necessary response to unfolding change and complexity in the range of achievements for which learners may seek recognition can be accommodated at unit level. The communication of these achievements in a clearly understood and accessible format is located at the level of the qualification.

There is another reason why the approval of rules of combination is a necessary point of intervention by the regulator in the process of quality assuring credit-based qualifications. This is because the rules of combination for qualifications are the devices through which the operational limitations of the credit system will be established. The approval of these rules of combination will therefore give the regulator the chance to ensure that individual qualifications offer the maximum range of opportunities for exploiting the potential of the credit system.

A combination of agreed structure, up-to-date guidance, examples of innovative practice and responsibility for approval will provide the regulator with the necessary range of interventions in developing rules of combination that will ensure that individual qualifications contribute effectively to the overall development of the framework for recognising achievement. Thus the regulators would use their powers to ensure that the broad interests of learners are served as well as the coherence and fitness-for-purpose of individual qualifications.

The processes of credit accumulation and transfer

Establishing approved rules of combination for each individual qualification establishes the basis for the operation of the processes of credit accumulation and transfer between qualifications and awarding bodies. Within these rules of combination a range of different arrangements for credit accumulation and transfer may operate. Some of these will be a requirement of awarding bodies as a condition of qualification approval. Others will fall within the discretion of awarding bodies to determine.

So, for example, all awarding bodies would be required to recognise the credits awarded by all other awarding bodies on any units referred to explicitly within the rules of combination of a qualification. Thus if unit x is referred to as either a core or an optional unit within a qualification offered by awarding body y, then the credits issued by awarding body z for that same unit would be automatically accepted by awarding body y, providing any time restrictions on the shelf life of units contained in the rules of combination for the qualification were adhered to. This 'mutual recognition of units' would meet one of the requirements of the DfES in relation to the credit framework.[31]

A manageable extension of this principle, and one that exploits the potential of the credit system to create stable measures of equivalence between different sets of learning outcomes, would be to create the obligation to recognise all credits offered at the same level on any unit bearing the same title. Thus, for example, a level one unit in word processing might offer learners the opportunity to earn three credits. These credits would then be transferable between all qualifications offering a three-credit unit at level one within their rules of combination. This facility would permit several units to be developed with the same title, credit value and level within the unit databank There would be no advantage to awarding bodies in continually creating variations around this unit title, as all variants would have equal value in terms of their potential for credit transfer, but some variations would prove useful in ensuring that units continued to be responsive to all possible demands.

It is therefore suggested that it is the mutual recognition of the credit value and level of units with the same title that should form the basis of the obligations of awarding bodies for mutual recognition. This facility will prevent the unnecessary duplication of units within the unit databank, as well as maximising credit transfer arrangements for useful variants on the same title as a feature of the framework.

Beyond this obligation, awarding bodies would also be encouraged to develop the widest possible set of opportunities for credit transfer between qualifications and awarding bodies. Providing the overall rules of combination are fit for the purpose for which the qualification is designed, the regulator will be in a position to encourage (rather than compel) awarding bodies to make maximum use of the potential of the credit system to offer qualifications responsive to individual needs. The example of the rules of combination outlined above illustrates some of these possibilities.

We may assume that, over time, those qualifications that create the maximum range of opportunities for credit transfer within their rules of combination will become those most favoured by both learners and by providers of learning opportunities. Thus a judicious combination of compulsion through regulation and encouragement through competition will stimulate a gradual realisation of the potential of credit-based qualifications to maximise opportunities for the recognition of learner achievement.

An inclusive framework for recognising learner achievement

Having identified some of the key technical issues to be addressed in the future, and noting the joint brief but very different roles of QCA and LSC in relation to the development of a credit framework for adults, how might the concepts of 'credit inside' and 'credit outside' the NQF relate to the expressed wish of QCA to create a single, inclusive Framework for Achievement?

It is suggested here that the practical experience of recognising learner achievements through credit-based awards has proved to be a more inclusive model than the recognition of achievement through qualifications within the NQF. Conversely, there is little doubt that qualifications within the NQF have proved themselves to be more effective than credit-based awards in securing formal recognition from employers, universities and others in relation to progression and employment opportunities for learners in the post-school sector.

The possibility is now opening up for these twin features of inclusiveness and currency to be brought together in a single framework for recognising achievement. If we are to develop a new FfA, based on the specifications for new credit-based qualifications, then qualifications and awards that currently sit inside and outside the NQF must be able to find a way into the new Framework. This creates an interesting problem of perception for the regulatory authorities who are charged with responsibility for maintaining standards within the existing NQF as well as leading development of this new Framework.

In this sense, the established history of credit outside the NQF provides a concrete and valid test of the capacity of the new FfA to encompass all formally recognised learner achievements. The question of whether or not a reformed NQF can become inclusive is not a theoretical case to be discussed, but a very practical proposition that will have an impact on the achievements of hundreds of thousands of adult learners. Having manifestly failed to achieve its ambition to be inclusive in its original format, the onus is clearly on a reformed NQF to demonstrate that it is able to incorporate into its architecture and operations those aspects of credit systems that can help it realise its ambition at the second attempt.

In this respect the joint remit for QCA and LSC will be useful. If the new Framework is to be genuinely new, then at the point when agreement is reached on the specifications of the FfA and the process for placing things within it, the Framework itself will be empty. From its inception therefore, the status of things 'inside' or 'outside' the existing NQF will be immaterial. All achievements need to be included within the new Framework, and therefore both QCA and LSC have a shared interest in ensuring that the FfA proceeds towards inclusiveness as it develops. For this reason it may be necessary for the concept of 'regulation' of credit-based qualifications to be shared in the interim between those bodies (QCA, QAA and possibly LSC itself) that have an existing interest in both credit and qualifications frameworks as structures for recognising achievement.

Such a 'framework merger' will take time, and the timescale for reform to 2010 envisaged by government seems realistic.[32] The acid test of inclusiveness needs to be applied continuously through this period of development. At those points at which the FfA demonstrates itself incapable of encompassing learner achievements currently recognised within credit systems, the regulator(s) of the Framework need to review the architecture and operations of the Framework to ensure it remains inclusive.

By 2010 we will therefore have a genuinely new and inclusive Framework, capable of responding flexibly and effectively to the changing demands of learners, employers and other users of qualifications. Or we will have a Framework that continues to exclude some achievements from recognition, and the concepts of 'credit inside' and 'credit outside' the NQF will still be with us.

Conclusion

This paper has selected six features of the architecture and operation of credit-based qualifications to illustrate how the technical features of such qualifications can be used to develop a flexible and potentially inclusive framework for recognising learner achievement. Although there are many other such features, it is suggested that these illustrative examples are sufficient for a paper that seeks to point out the potential connections between principles and technical specifications that will form the basis of work on the development of credit-based qualifications in the immediate future.

The principle of 'regulation for inclusion' lies at the heart of these proposals. It will be possible in theory to develop a Framework for Achievement through credit-based qualifications that can meet the desire of policy-makers that the NQF can be transformed into such an inclusive framework. To meet this objective, while maintaining the stability of the credit as a currency of achievement within a qualifications framework that is intelligible to all users will be a major challenge. But it can be done. It is hoped that this paper shows some ways in which we can do it.

Notes

1. *21st Century Skills: Realising our Potential*, DfES, July 2003.
2. Through the jointly chaired LSC/QCA Framework and Credit Group.
3. *Modularisation and credit accumulation and transfer*, Coombe Lodge paper 1989.
4. Conference organised by the Further Education Campaign Group and the Forum for Access Studies, Coventry, November 1991.
5. *A Basis for Credit?* Further Education Unit, 1992.
6. Statement issued by the Association for Colleges and five other professional associations: *A National Credit Framework*, July 1992, Association of Colleges *et al.*
7. Submission by John Hillier (Chief Executive of NCVQ) to the House of Commons Post-16 Education Committee *Towards a national system of credit accumulation*, a discussion paper, May 1993.
8. *Beyond a Basis for Credit* FEU, 1993.
9. *Annual Report 1998-99* National Open College Network, 1999.
10. Kennedy, H. *Learning works – widening participation in Further Education* FEFC 1997.
11. Fryer, R. *Learning for the twenty-first century*, first report of the National Advisory Group for Continuing Education and Lifelong Learning, 1997.
12. Dearing, R. *Review of qualifications for 16-19 year-olds*, SCAA, 1996.
13. *Education Act*, DfEE, 1997.
14. *Statistical Review 2002-03*, LSC.
15. *QCA Quinquennial Review 2002*, QCA, 2002.
16. *Blackstone Announces A Level improvements*, DfEE press release 170/98, 1998.
17. For example, the winding up of the Derbyshire Regional Network and the demise of the London Credit Framework.
18. *Annual Report 2002-03*, National Open College Network, 2003.
19. Although LSDA has produced some publications on credit, there is nothing to compare to the set of technical documents and discussion papers produced by both FEU and FEDA. The support of NIACE for the development of OCNs and for NOCN itself was not continued after 1999.
20. In addition to the resignation of Ron McClone as Chief Executive of OCR, and Bill Stubbs as Chief Executive of QCA in the autumn of 2002, Estelle Morris resigned as Secretary of State for Education in October 2002 partly as a result of the A Level debacle.
21. Ken Boston was actually appointed to the post of Chief Executive of QCA before the events of summer 2002, but took up this position immediately following the resignation of Bill Stubbs.
22. *14–19 Curriculum and Qualifications Reform* Interim Report of the Working Group on 14-19 Reform, February 2004.
23. *The National Credit Framework*, National Open College Network, 1994.
24. The Access to Higher Education Recognition Scheme, now the responsibility of the Quality Assurance Agency for Higher Education, has produced a number of Access to HE Certificates that could serve as a model for credit-based qualifications across the Learning and Skills sector.
25. *New thinking for Reform: A Framework for Achievement*, QCA, July 2004.
26. *Credit principles for England*, QCA, March 2004.
27. More information about the Scottish Credit and Qualifications Framework is available at www.scqf.org.uk.

28. Other databases that may provide useful models for development include the learndirect database of courses and several unit databases, the most useful of which can be found at www.units.org.uk.

29. See *The statutory regulation of external qualifications in England, Wales and Northern Ireland* QCA, ACCAC and CCEA 2004 and also QCA's new five-day accreditation model.

30. All Sector Skills Councils will be required to establish a Sector Qualifications Strategy as a condition of their initial core funding.

31. In *21st Century Skills* there is an explicit reference in the section on qualifications reform (Chapter 5) to 'the mutual recognition of units' as a key feature of a reformed system.

32. In *New Thinking for Reform* (*ibid*) the timetable for reform extends to 2010. The interim proposals for development of the proposed reforms of the Tomlinson Group envisage a timescale stretching until 2014.